D1710276

j355.12
men

✪ WEAPONS OF WAR
UNIFORMS
1944 TO TODAY

HOMEWOOD PUBLIC LIBRARY

FEB -- 2015

Smart Apple Media

© 2015 Smart Apple Media, an imprint of Black Rabbit Books
P.O. Box 3263, Mankato, Minnesota, 56002
www.blackrabbitbooks.com

All rights reserved. No part of this publication may be reproduced,
stored in a retrieval system, or transmitted, in any form or by any means,
electronic, mechanical, photocopying, recording, or otherwise, without
prior written permission from the publisher.

Published by arrangement with Amber Books

Contributing authors: Chris Chant, Steve Crawford, Martin J. Dougherty,
Ian Hogg, Robert Jackson, Chris McNab, Michael Sharpe, Philip Trewhitt

Special thanks to series consultant Dr. Steve Potts

Photo credits: Art-Tech/Aerospace, Cody Images, Corbis, U.S. Department of Defense

Illustrations: © Art-Tech/Aerospace

Library of Congress Cataloging-in-Publication Data

McNab, Chris, 1970-
Uniforms : 1944 to today / Chris McNab.
pages cm. — (Weapons of war)
ISBN 978-1-62588-048-2
1. Military uniforms — History — 20th century. 2. Military uniforms — History — 21st century. I. Title.
UC480.M378 2015
355.1'4--dc23
                              2013032036

Printed in the United States at Corporate Graphics,
North Mankato, Minnesota
PO1649
2-2014

9 8 7 6 5 4 3 2 1

CONTENTS

Introduction

An Era of Camouflage

Military uniforms in the second half of the twentieth century were designed to be practical and offer the soldier some concealment.

The historical study of military uniforms has a broader significance than is commonly appreciated. A military uniform, after all, signals the practical, regimental, even ideological priorities of the soldier on the battlefield. Thus, as we review the history of military clothing, we see not only the display of regimental pride, but also a barometer for the changes in warfare itself. Shifts in battlefield technology and tactics have demanded new modes of dress and equipment and new ways of understanding the nature of armed conflict.

Uniforms as we understand them today — standardized items of dress issued to formations or armies — are actually quite a recent phenomenon. Roman, Greek, Byzantine and other ancient armies certainly had comparable aspects to their appearance, including the use of specific colors to signal unit membership, but this was not the

US MARINES, KOREA: see page 54

NORTH KOREAN PRISONERS: see page 40

general policy. During the Middle Ages, some formations, such as knights loyal to a particular lord or the Janissaries of the Ottoman army, would strike a common form of dress, but this was often more to do with tribal or social loyalties rather than militarized clothing. Individual improvisation in clothing was common.

THE BIRTH OF UNIFORMS

Military uniforms are largely the creation of the 17th century, as the birth of the regimental system (initially in France) brought with it the issue of dress regulations. It took until the establishment of standing armies for this system to become permanent. Beginning with the eighteenth century, it became typical for soldiers to wear common, regulated uniforms, designed with unit, formation and branch allegiance designated. Naval uniforms were also established in the eighteenth century, although many navies only dictated officer dress until the mid-1800s.

Until the late nineteenth century, and even beyond, the uniforms of land armies paid little attention to the principles of camouflage and concealment we so value today. The bright colors, headgear, and flashy braids, tassels and plumes worn declared open pride and tradition. (The plainer uniforms of the Civil War provided a notable exception.) The twentieth century would change the situation dramatically.

NORTH VIETNAMESE ARMY, 1954: see page 41

CUBAN GUERRILLAS: see page 29

WEAPONS OF WAR

FRENCH PARATROOPERS: see page 31

THE TWO WORLD WARS

By the 1890s, breech-loading weapons (both artillery and firearms) had made the battlefield an increasingly deadly place. Steadily, uniforms began to lose their dramatic colors, becoming plainer to serve purposes of utility and basic camouflage — increasingly, to be visible was to be dead. Logistics alone demanded standardization of uniforms. Ornate uniforms simply could not be produced with the necessary speed, quantity, or economy to equip the new mass armies. The hordes of soldiers who entered World War I were mainly dressed in plain tunics and trousers, although many older regiments distinguished themselves with the brighter and more defiant uniforms from the past. The cavalry were particularly vivid. Germany, for example, had various cavalry units, each wearing bright regimental tunics, trousers, and tall head-dress, such as the shako. World War I cemented the changes and, by the end of the conflict, most troops were dressed in plain olive-drab or grey uniforms, with their equipment carried in utilitarian webbing systems. The advent of

US GREEN BERETS: see page 55

WEAPONS OF WAR

PAKISTANI INFANTRY: see page 42

air power also established an entirely new pattern of service dress.

During the interwar period camouflage for soldiers truly took hold. In 1929, the Italian Army issued a camouflaged tent-cloth called the *tela mimetizzata* (camouflaged cloth) and, in 1930, the German forces produced a triangular poncho/tent sheet called a *Zeltbahn*. The pattern derived from this was called *Zeltbahn* 31 and consisted of green and brown angular shapes against a tan background, with short, rain-like green streaks breaking up the lines in a dense pattern. This became known as *Splittertarn* (splinter) pattern, which was used on World

War II uniforms issued for some German soldiers.

World War II brought change as well as continuity. Camouflage designed specifically to break up the silhouette of the soldier was introduced and numerous specialist uniforms emerged for different technological roles, from paratroopers to bomber pilots. Nazi Germany was to stay at the forefront of camouflage uniform design, far ahead of any other army. The Waffen-SS in particular was a pioneer, especially through the input of SS-Sturmbannführer Wim Brandt and his assistant Professor Otto Schick. Starting in 1937 they produced a range of foliage-

WEAPONS OF WAR

BIAFRAN SOLDIERS: see page 25

MOZAMBIQUE 1970: see page 43

pattern camouflage patterns (mainly the *Platanenmuster* (plane tree), *Palmenmuster* (palm tree) and *Eichenlaubmuster* (oak leaf), which closely imitated nature. These uniforms were later estimated to reduce unit casualties by 15 percent in combat.

POST-WAR DEVELOPMENTS

Following the war, advanced technologies steadily transformed uniforms and personal load-carrying equipment in modern armies. During the second half of the twentieth century, standardization continued on a global scale. There are two primary causes. First, at the end of WW II massive amounts of war surplus were released, especially in former European colonies. Thus, British

Army khaki was worn in places as disparate as Greece, India, Pakistan, Iraq, Africa, and Malaysia well into the 1970s, with the British 1938-pattern webbing still in use in many places today.

Second, the onset of the Cold War started a global chess game in which the United States, the Soviet Union, and China sponsored various proxy wars with military supplies. For example, South Korean soldiers in the 1950s could be seen in US M1943 combat uniform, while their North Korean opponents would be in Chinese khaki uniforms.

These two forces of standardization exercised their influence worldwide, not only making soldiers within nations look the same or similar, but also making soldiers of different

INDIA 1971: see page 35

The US M1943 uniform became the basis for a whole range of uniforms developed by new armed forces in the postwar era.

nations resemble one another. The growth of guerrilla warfare in the post-war world has also meant that we see items from various Cold War military sources in unlikely combination, as revolutionary fighters or terrorists used whatever military stock was available.

In the post-war period, it became apparent that wealth has become the defining factor in the sophistication of uniforms. Today, many developing countries in the Middle East and Africa have uniforms similar to those seen during World War II, but the same cannot be said for the developed world. The United States set the standard in WW II with its M1943 uniform. This adopted a layered

approach to uniforms, based on the principle that many thin layers give better temperature control than few thick ones.

The success of the M1943 model caught on, and the UK and other European countries began either buying the uniform direct or developing versions of their own. From this point on — particularly from the 1960s — the world's developed nations moved ahead with uniform design at a rapid rate. By the 1970s, camouflage had become standard in many nations: the UK with its Disruptive Pattern Material (DPM); the US its special forces with "Tigerstripe" in Vietnam, later using the M81 Woodland pattern for most soldiers in the US

WEAPONS OF WAR

EGYPTIAN SOLDIERS 1967: see page 30

Army; the Soviet Union having its "jigsaw" and leaf patterns.

COLD WAR UNIFORMS

From the 1960s in particular, advanced materials, refined camouflages, and ergonomic webbing systems gave soldiers a level of comfort and practicality as never before. Customization was a major feature of many US soldiers' equipment and uniform throughout the Vietnam War. Many troops made adaptations using local sources and adding their own artwork and slogans. Following the troubled Vietnam War period, the US armed forces substantially reinvented themselves during the 1980s, renewing their tactics and much of their equipment.

Despite World War II being over, the same style of uniform dominated Soviet infantry until well into the 1960s. A replacement uniform was put into use about 1970, when the Soviet Army began modernizing. During the 1970s and 1980s, camouflage uniforms started to be introduced in greater quantities

MUJAHEDEEN 1980: see page 22

WEAPONS OF WAR

IRANIAN REVOLUTIONARIES 1980: see page 36

SOUTH AFRICAN SOLDIER 1980: see page 45

into the Soviet Army, particularly for special forces and operational units in war zones. When not wearing the *ushanka* fur cap, Soviet troops in the late 1980s would generally wear either the SSh-40 or newer SSh-60 helmet, or a simple forage cap that replaced the *pilotka* sidecap in 1984. However, troops could also be seen in broad-brimmed, officer-style caps.

The 1980s brought significant changes to British Army uniform and equipment.

Not least of these changes was the replacement of the time-proven L1A1 rifle with the 5.56mm SA80/L85A1 as the standard British Army rifle. The 1990s continued the trend of uniform and equipment changes in the British armed forces. The layered-principle, lightweight Combat Soldier 95 (CS95) uniform replaced the previous DPM No. 8 and 9 Dress.

ARGENTINIAN MARINES 1982: see page 24

By 1950, over 350 different types of camouflage uniforms were being used throughout the world.

THE MODERN ERA

By 1990, more than 350 camouflages were in use throughout the world (a large percentage in the modern Russia and the former Soviet republics). Some of these are increasingly sophisticated, British and US uniforms even incorporate anti-reflective dyes to confuse night-vision scopes. Materials such as Gore-Tex, which allows perspiration to evaporate while keeping out rainwater, make advanced jackets for the modern combat soldier, while boots made of similar materials have reduced common medical conditions such as trench

foot. Load-carrying systems are now no longer based purely on belt and straps. For example, the US Army's Integrated Individual Fighting System places most of its pouches on the back and front of a close-fitting vest, keeping weight more aligned over the body's center of gravity.

The economics of the modern world has meant that armies have become smaller and smaller in many countries, yet operational demands require that each soldier receives more per person in terms of equipment than soldiers of 60 years ago. With the concern of

BRITISH AVIATOR: see page 49

ISRAELI DEFENSE FORCE, LEBANON 1982: see page 39

WEAPONS OF WAR

BRAZILIAN UNITED NATIONS SOLDIER: see page 26

public response to casualties in conflict — a primary political fear in the US following the Vietnam War and more recent conflicts in Iraq and Afghanistan — investments are made in the world's wealthier countries to give each soldier the best survival chance possible.

Modern armed forces are better equipped today than at any point in history. Weapons are more powerful and less prone to failure and uniforms have been designed around advanced ergonomic principles. The US Army uniform of the early twenty-first century, for example, uses the Universal Camouflage Pattern (UCP), a pattern designed to provide basic camouflage in urban, temperate woodland, and desert environments. Soldiers carry their equipment on an Improved Outer Tactical Vest (IOTV) system. These uniforms make the experience of carrying heavy loads and surviving under adverse climates as bearable as possible.

So what of the future? New trends are already emerging: uniforms using camouflage materials that change, chameleon-like, with the terrain and background; helmets with built-in computer screens for viewing real-time tactical information; self-heating/chilling fabrics that enable the same uniform to be worn in different climates. There are even new materials currently entering the market that generate an electrical charge via the soldier's movements, which are sufficient to power equipment without the need for external power supply. It's clear that the uniforms of tomorrow will do far more than just protect the body.

AFGHANISTAN

Guerrilla Fighter, Mujahedeen, Afghanistan, 1980

As is typical of guerrilla fighters the world over, dress often tends to be civilian for both reasons of availability and the tactical advantages of an anonymous appearance. Here the jacket and calf-length trousers are made from local cloth and the sandals from riveted leather, both to traditional designs. More ceremonial elements of dress include the traditional head-dress and blue sash wrapped around the upper body. No webbing is worn, and all supplies are carried in the musette bag hung over one shoulder. The weapon is a bolt-action hunting rifle, but, as the war progressed, the guerrillas were often seen with more advanced arms, either captured from the Soviets or US-supplied (mainly AK rifles) being shipped over the Pakistan/Afghan border. The Mujahedeen did an effective job of battling the Soviet occupation and destroying morale among the occupying troops.

SPECIFICATIONS
DATE: 1980
UNIT: Mujahedeen
RANK: Guerrilla Fighter
THEATRE: Afghanistan
LOCATION: Afghan mountains

Guerrilla fighter, Taliban Militia, Afghanistan, 2001

This Taliban fighter wears the ad hoc mix of clothing typical of guerrilla forces the world over. The long, white shalwar kameez is a classic two-piece item of Afghan clothing, and a blue jipped jacket is worn over the top. The outer layer, however, is a basic camouflage jacket, although it is uncertain whether this is military surplus or a civilian brand. Footwear is nothing more than a pair of civilian shoes, which would have limited durability in Afghanistan's mountainous areas. Much of the Taliban's military clothing has been appropriated from foreign armies, including those of the Soviet Union and Pakistan, which is where many of the Taliban's arms originate. As expected, this soldier has an AKM rifle, fitted with a folding stock.

SPECIFICATIONS
DATE: October 2001
UNIT: Taliban Militia
RANK: Guerrilla Fighter
THEATRE: Afghanistan
LOCATION: Jalalabad

Senior Sergeant, Argentine Marines, Falklands, 1982

During the Falklands War in 1980, the arctic conditions of the South Atlantic posed a challenge to British and Argentine forces alike. Though standards of uniform wavered throughout the Argentine Army, this NCO has good clothing for the environment (the Argentine Marines tended to receive a higher quality of winter uniform than regular units). He wears a thermal parka jacket: padded, windproof and waterproof, with a deep hood capable of going over the helmet. The helmet is of US supply, as is the webbing and ammunition pouches on the belt (more ammunition is carried in the two bandoliers hung over the shoulders). As the US was a major supplier of military stock to Argentina, a US Army appearance is typical among its forces, but the blue-and-white patch above the red rank chevrons on the chest clearly defines nationality. The soldier carries eye goggles for protection against the weather.

SPECIFICATIONS

DATE: 1982
UNIT: Argentine Marines
RANK: Senior Sergeant
THEATRE: Falkland Islands
LOCATION: East Falkland

Private, Biafran Army, East Nigeria, 1968

The Biafran Army fought an independence war for three years (1967–70) against the much more powerful and well-equipped Nigerian Army. Though they performed well as individuals, the Biafrans suffered from a chronic lack of equipment and took military supplies from a range of sources, both military and civilian, a situation evident in the soldier here. His shirt and jacket are unknown, though probably taken from the Soviet-supplied kit that flooded many countries of Africa during the Cold War period. The wellington boots are civilian, hardly suitable or comfortable footwear for the African heat. He wears a soft cap, though Biafran soldiers can be seen in a variety of US and Soviet helmets during the conflict. For armament, a 7.62mm Vz.58 assault rifle is carried — a Czech copy of the Kalashnikov AK47 — and a single large ammunition pouch for the 30-round magazines is strapped on his left hip.

SPECIFICATIONS

DATE: 1968
UNIT: Biafran Army
RANK: Private
THEATRE: West Africa
LOCATION: East Nigeria

Brazilian UN Peacekeeper, UNTAET, East Timor, 2001

The United Nations Transitional Administration in East Timor (UNTAET) was established in 1999 to oversee East Timor's pained transition to independence. It put in place a multinational peacekeeping force, which included the soldier seen here. Brazil's armed forces have adopted a variety of camouflage patterns, mostly based around foliage patterns (well-suited to Brazil's natural landscape, which includes dense jungles). This soldier has a variety of webbing pouches, including two zip-fastened thigh bags and he also has knee protectors, always useful when spending large amounts of time crouched or lying by the sides of roads. His UN status is denoted by the blue helmet and the shoulder and belt patches and his weapon is a folding-stock version of the popular FN FAL rifle.

SPECIFICATIONS
DATE: December 2001
UNIT: UNTAET
RANK: Private
THEATRE: Southeast Asia
LOCATION: Dili, East Timor

Warrant Officer, Princess Patricia's Light Infantry, Cyprus 1970s

For the early part of the post-World War II period, Canada followed the British Army models of kit and dress. However, the Canadian military soon began to forge its own identity and leaned more toward the United States model. This soldier of the Princess Patricia's Light Infantry — one of Canada's most prestigious units, formed in 1914 — is at an interesting juncture. His weapon is the British Army's L1A1 Self-Loading Rifle and his uniform standard Canadian olive-drab. The webbing is based on the US ALICE system, worn with two ammunition/utility pouches. Since then, most forms of kit have become indigenous. The L1A1 was replaced by the C7, a Canadian adaptation of the US M16 rifle, while the latest Improved Environmental Clothing System (IECS), Load Carriage System and Tactical Vest form a superb, home-grown battlefield kit.

SPECIFICATIONS
DATE: 1970s
UNIT: Princess Patricia's Light Infantry
RANK: Warrant Officer
THEATRE: Mediterranean
LOCATION: Cyprus

C

CHINA

Private, Chinese People's Liberation Army, Korea, 1951

Only a year into the existence of the new Communist state, Chinese forces were once again in combat, this time assisting Communist North Korea in its attempted take-over of UN-backed South Korea. Over the three years of the Korean War, however, the PLA would lose up to one million men, despite early victories over the United Nations forces. The soldier's dress here gives some indication of the severity of the Korean climate. Arctic conditions could prevail in winter, thus he wears a fully quilted jacket and trousers, though the archaic puttees have remained. The cap is fur-lined, with extensive ear flaps to prevent frostbite; his footwear does not suggest as much protection. Ammunition for his Type 88 Hanyang rifle is held in cotton bandoliers across the chest, which were popular in East Asian countries.

SPECIFICATIONS
DATE: 1951
UNIT: Chinese People's Liberation Army
RANK: Private
THEATRE: East Asia
LOCATION: South Korea

WEAPONS OF WAR

CUBA

Guerrilla, Cuban Revolutionary Forces, 1959

The Cuban Revolutionary Forces suffered from a lack of military supplies during the campaign to overthrow the government of Fulgencio Batista, yet intelligent and persistent tactics often made up for this. North American weapons and clothing were the primary fighting kit. Underneath his civilian jacket — emblazoned with a revolutionary Cuban patch — is a standard US herringbone-twill combat uniform. Worn by US Marines and Army soldiers during the Pacific campaign of World War II and the Korean War, it was hard-wearing and comfortable. The webbing is US-type, but the small ammunition pouches on the belt were for holding five-round clips for the M1 Garand semi-automatic rifle, whereas this revolutionary holds an older Springfield M1903 bolt-action firearm. The patch on his arm and beret are typical of guerrilla fighters.

SPECIFICATIONS

DATE: 1959
UNIT: Cuban Revolutionary Forces
RANK: Guerrilla Fighter
THEATRE: Cuba
LOCATION: Havana

Private, Egyptian Army Commandos, Sinai, 1967

By 1967, during which Israel launched the lightning Six-Day War on its immediate Arab neighbors, Cold War sponsorship of the conflict in the Middle East had broadly settled into Soviet backing for the Arab armies and Western backing for Israel. Though this Egyptian soldier is mostly equipped with local uniform and equipment, the Soviet influence is seen in the Russian infantryman's helmet and also the gas-mask pack, which can just be seen on the left hip. The other item on the belt is actually an aberration — a US water bottle in an M1941 cover — one which illustrates that many Arab soldiers had to innovate in how they put together their kit. The uniform is an Egyptian-made desert-camouflage tunic and trousers. The weapon is the Egyptian Port Said submachine gun, a copy of the Swedish 9mm Carl Gustav, made under licence in Egypt.

SPECIFICATIONS
DATE: 1967
UNIT: Egyptian Army Commandos
RANK: Private
THEATRE: Middle East
LOCATION: Sinai

Private, French 10th Parachute Division, Algeria, 1961

The Algerian Independence War demonstrated how effective and brutal, the French paras could be within a civil war/ revolutionary conflict. Between 1957 — when the 10th Parachute Division and 3rd Colonial Parachute Regiment were deployed — and July 1962, when Algeria achieved its independence, the paras perfected a style of counter-insurgency warfare that inflicted terrible losses on the nationalist ALN movement. Ultimately, it was their use of torture and murder that was their undoing, as the French military became vilified by the international press. This private is carrying a 7.5mm M1952 (AAT Mle 52) machine gun, a good attrition weapon for sudden encounters and he is wearing the standard M51 tropical parachute uniform. By this time, all French troops were wearing camouflage, a change that occurred in 1960.

SPECIFICATIONS
DATE: 1961
UNIT: 10th Parachute Division
RANK: Private
THEATRE: North Africa
LOCATION: Near Tunisian border

Private, Hitlerjugend Division, Normandy, 1944

By 1944, camouflage was making widespread appearance in many German units, though mainly those units with elite status. While much of this camouflage was confined to the Eastern Front initially, the threat of a second front in France forced Hitler to relocate some SS units there. This Hitlerjugend trooper is wearing an Italian pattern camouflage smock and trousers, the helmet also being covered in a matching cloth. The period 1944–45 saw many German units adopting surplus Italian military clothing, as Germany's own supplies ran short and industry could not produce enough to meet demand. This accounts for an increasing lack of consistent appearance among German troops on all fronts. The Hitlerjugend division was largely formed from former members of the Hitler Youth. This trooper is armed with the MG42 machine gun.

SPECIFICATIONS
DATE: June 1944
UNIT: Hitlerjugend Division
RANK: Private
THEATRE: Northwest Europe
LOCATION: Normandy

Senior Sergeant, 916th Infantry Regiment, Normandy, 1944

This image of a German Feldwebel (sergeant) shows the equipment carried by German infantry soldiers in 1944. The most recognizable item is the cylindrical gas mask case. This was made of fluted steel and featured a hinged lid containing additional eyepieces for the mask. Beneath this to right is the tent quarter/poncho known as the Zeltbahn 31, rendered in the distinctive Splitter (splinter) camouflage designed for army use in the 1930s. The Zeltbahn could be used as a wind shelter, a tent, a poncho, or even be made into an emergency stretcher. The two remaining items around the soldier's back are a canvas bread bag and a water bottle in leather cover. On the belt can be seen an ammunition pouch for his Mauser rifle. The rest of the uniform is standard German issue for this stage of the war, while the helmet has a wire cover for attaching camouflage.

SPECIFICATIONS
DATE: 6 June 1944
UNIT: 916th Infantry Regiment
RANK: Senior Sergeant
THEATRE: Northwest Europe
LOCATION: Normandy

G

Operative, GSG-9 Anti-Terrorist Unit, Germany, 1990s

The Grenzschutzgruppe-9 (GSG-9) ranks alongside the SAS Counter-Revolutionary Warfare team as one of the best hostage-rescue and anti-terrorist units in the world. Their formation was inspired by the débâcle at Munich in 1972, when a botched police rescue-attempt resulted in nine kidnapped Israeli athletes at the Munich Olympics being massacred by their captors. GSG-9 was established to create an efficient, standardized response force to national emergencies. Here we see an operative in classic urban-combat gear, with the suggestion of a helicopter deployment lying in his airborne harness for fast-roping down to buildings. His helmet is para-style, the high-side sections allowing good hearing, while a balaclava protects anonymity. His weapon, the 9mm HK MP5A3, is the choice of HRU teams world-wide for its stopping power.

SPECIFICATIONS

DATE: 1990s
UNIT: Grenzschutzgruppe-9
RANK: Operative
THEATRE: Europe
LOCATION: Germany

Private, Indian Army Paratrooper, East Pakistan, 1971

During India's invasion of East Pakistan in 1971, the Indian Army relied on its airborne forces to make rapid assaults and take the East Pakistan forces by surprise. Occupation of the region was achieved in only 12 days. This para has moved on from the khaki battledress of the 1960s, but the British influence remains, albeit in an updated form. He mostly wears British parachute clothing, including the Denison jump-smock in DPM (Disruptive Pattern Material), which features the white parachute with blue wings brevet on a khaki field. The helmet is also British para issue. Over the smock is the 1937-pattern webbing system, superseded by the 1958-pattern in the British Army, but still a good way of load-carrying. The pouches hold 30-round magazines for the 7.62mm L1A1 rifle, here with its short knife bayonet.

SPECIFICATIONS
DATE: 1971
UNIT: Indian Army
RANK: Private
THEATRE: Indo-Pakistan War
LOCATION: East Pakistan

Private, Iranian Revolutionary Guard Corps, Iran/Iraq Border, 1980

The Iranian Revolutionary Guard Corps, also known as the Pasdarin, has been at the vanguard of Iran's armed operations for the last three decades and consequently has seen massive losses. A horrific death toll during the eight-year war with neighboring Iraq (1980–88) was something from which Iranian forces never completely recovered. Despite the decimation, however, the Revolutionary Guard still remains one of the Tehran regime's most capable resources. This soldier is pictured in 1980 at the beginning of hostilities with Iraq. The uniform of simple khaki fatigues is the same as that of the pre-revolutionary army, while the webbing is British in type, the helmet the US M1 and the weapon the German Heckler & Koch G3. The mix of sources shown here indicates the supply difficulties always experienced by Iran.

SPECIFICATIONS
DATE: 1980
UNIT: Iranian Revolutionary Guard Corps
RANK: Private
THEATRE: Middle East
LOCATION: Iran–Iraq border

IRAQ

Private, Republican Guard, Iraqi Army, Iraq, 1991

The main distinguishing features of the Iraqi Republican Guard in the early 1990s, at least on the regular combat uniform, were the red triangular sleeve patch (often worn on both sleeves) and the matching beret. Other than that, the soldier here wears the typical uniform of the Iraqi army — a wool/synthetic blend shirt and trousers, the former featuring two large chest pockets (although there could be variations in the number of pockets). Personal items, or possibly mapwork, are carried in a simple canvas shoulder bag. His weapon is the Iraqi-produced version of the AK-47, known as the Tabuk. Like the original it copied, the Tabuk gave excellent and resilient service in the hard desert conditions.

SPECIFICATIONS

DATE: February 1991
UNIT: Iraqi Republican Guard
RANK: Private
THEATRE: Persian Gulf
LOCATION: Iraq

UNIFORMS: 1944 TO TODAY

Fighter, Fedayeen Saddam Militia, Baghdad, 2003

The Fedayeen Saddam was essentially Saddam Hussein's own personal paramilitary force, located outside the conventional army's chain of command and numbering upwards of 40,000 personnel. With a name meaning "Saddam's Men of Sacrifice", they were used for personal security "solutions" by Saddam's regime (particularly by his brother, Uday) before the 2003 invasion of Iraq and thereafter prosecuted a guerrilla war against the Americans, British and their allies. The white uniform here was largely ceremonial and was indicative of their sacrificial rationale — in actual combat many would fight in either regular combat uniforms or civilian clothing. Ammunition for the soldier's AKM rifle is carried in a three-pouch chest webbing system, and he wears standard-issue Iraqi Army leather boots.

SPECIFICATIONS
DATE: March 2003
UNIT: Fedayeen Saddam
RANK: n/a
THEATRE: Iraq
LOCATION: Baghdad, Iraq

ISRAEL

Corporal, 202nd Parachute Brigade, Lebanon, 1982

This Israeli soldier patrolling in the Lebanon is wearing the standard olive-green field uniform of the Israel Defense Forces (IDF), capped by a ballistic-nylon helmet that acted as the replacement for the old steel variety. The webbing is also Israeli issue, and can be distinguished from foreign supply by the "boot-lace" fittings connecting the straps to the belt. What is more notable about this soldier is his weaponry as, prepared for the dangerous possibilities of a street patrol in the Lebanon, he carries a 5.56mm Galil assault rifle, produced in Israel in response to dissatisfaction with Israeli small arms during the Yom Kippur War. An excellent, reliable weapon with a bolt-action, it was based on the Kalashnikov rifles. The soldier carries IMI bullet-trap rifle-grenades for the Galil, most likely with high explosive or tear-gas warheads for urban combat.

SPECIFICATIONS
DATE: 1982
UNIT: 202nd Parachute Brigade
RANK: Corporal
THEATRE: Middle East
LOCATION: South Lebanon

Private, Korean People's Army, Pyongyang, 1950

In contrast to many United Nations troops in the early years of the Korean War, this soldier is extremely well-dressed for the severe Korean winter climate. His jacket and trousers are made from thickly quilted material, the jacket featuring a double-breasted design with zipper fastening to reduce penetration by wind chill. The hat is similarly judicious, as the ear flaps would have prevented the frostbite that afflicted many troops in the sub-zero winter months. Note the complete absence of rank or markings on this cold-weather gear; the normal uniform — based on Soviet patterns — would have rank on the shoulder-straps and the collar. The Soviet weapon is a 7.62mm PPSh41, here fitted with a 71-round drum magazine. Though this soldier is well equipped, a North Korean soldier's life was one of terrible austerity.

SPECIFICATIONS
DATE: 1950
UNIT: Korean People's Army
RANK: Private
THEATRE: East Asia
LOCATION: Pyongyang

Private, North Vietnamese Army, Hanoi, 1954

This soldier is seen during the victory celebrations in Hanoi following the collapse of French forces in Indochina after their cataclysmic defeat during the 55-day siege at Dien Bien Phu. The experience the NVA had gained in revolutionary war would stand them in good stead for the forthcoming conflict with South Vietnam and the United States. The appearance of this soldier is essentially little different from that of NVA soldiers in that later conflict. The olive-drab uniform is probably of local origin, the ankles of the trousers featuring buttons to keep out the insect life of the jungle floor. He holds aloft a hat made from woven reeds covered with cloth, little physical protection in itself, but cooling in the Vietnamese climate. His web belt holds a water bottle and a machete, while his rifle is a captured French 7.5mm MAS 1936.

SPECIFICATIONS

DATE: 1954
UNIT: North Vietnamese Army
RANK: Private
THEATRE: Southeast Asia
LOCATION: Hanoi

Private, Pakistani Army, West Pakistan, 1971

Even by the 1970s, British equipment and dress were still one of the dominant presences in the military forces of the Indian subcontinent. In Pakistan, however, economic constraints meant that this presence was mixed with a whole host of other sources. This soldier is wearing the US M1 steel helmet, but the webbing system is the British Army 1958-pattern. The uniform itself is the Pakistani khaki drill tunic and trousers, this being worn with a V-neck pullover in olive-green, which, despite its informal appearance, was a regular item of Pakistani uniform. A piece of equipment that was definitely not of military origin is the canvas shopping bag. The soldier pictured here is using it to carry around some personal effects for which there isn't a proper pouch or backpack. Rank in the Pakistani Army would be displayed on the upper sleeve for the NCOs or on the shoulder-straps for officers.

SPECIFICATIONS

DATE: 1971
UNIT: Pakistani Army
RANK: Private
THEATRE: South Asia
LOCATION: West Pakistan

Corporal, Portuguese Parachute Regiment, Mozambique, 1970

The post-war period signaled an intense struggle for Portugal to retain its African possessions, a struggle that lasted well into the 1970s in places such as Guinea-Bissau, Angola and Mozambique. Thus Portugal's armed forces gained a huge wealth of experience in counter-insurgency warfare. This is a corporal of the Portuguese Parachute Regiment, a unit typical of the élite forces usually used in Portugal's colonial conflicts. He wears a 1950 French pattern of camouflage in a distinctive green, brown and olive-green color scheme. On a practical combat uniform, there is a minimum of insignia. The rank is displayed by the two chevrons on each shoulder slide; membership of the Parachute Regiment is depicted through the para badge on the right breast. The beret badge is that of the Portuguese Air Force.

SPECIFICATIONS
DATE: 1970
UNIT: Portuguese Parachute Regiment
RANK: Corporal
THEATRE: Southern Africa
LOCATION: Mozambique

Private, Spetsnaz, Russian Army, Chechnya, 1995

The Spetsnaz soldier here is wearing an R91 flora pattern camouflage uniform, which featured six large pockets and a spacious detachable hood. He has matching combat trousers, tucked into a simple pair of 12-eyelet leather combat boots. There is no visible rank on the uniform — particularly for officers, open displays of rank were not advisable in the presence of so many capable Chechen snipers. This soldier has the standard AKM rifle, unlike many Special Forces operatives who used the more modern 5.45mm AK74. It was common to see soldiers in Chechnya shunning the standard Russian Army helmet and replacing it with a simple (and much warmer) woolen hat, as seen here.

SPECIFICATIONS

DATE: April 1995
UNIT: Spetsnaz
RANK: Private
THEATRE: Caucasus
LOCATION: Grozny, Chechnya

Private, South African Army, Namibia, 1980

South Africa fought a long and bitter counter-insurgency conflict within Namibia from the late 1960s to 1988, the date on which Namibia achieved full independence from South Africa, even though it had been granted this in theory by the UN in 1966. Combat against the South West African People's Organization (SWAPO), mainly based in Angola, was a hot affair, so uniforms tended towards simplicity and light materials. This soldier wears a cotton two-piece khaki uniform, the shirt and trousers having the additional feature of covered pocket buttons to stop the buttons snagging on foliage when on patrol. His webbing system priorities are food and water. Around the back would be a water bottle centered on the belt and flanked by two kidney pouches for rations, survival gear and personal effects. To the front are two large ammunition pouches, each holding two magazines for his FN FAL rifle.

SPECIFICATIONS
DATE: 1980
UNIT: South African Army
RANK: Private
THEATRE: Southern Africa
LOCATION: Namibia

Private, Army of the Republic of Korea, South Korea, 1951

South Korea's Army lost around 45 percent of all its troops in the first three months of the Korean War, such was the state of its structure, equipment and morale. UN military support and US equipment saved it from an even more ignominious fate at the hands of the North Koreans. This soldier shows his indebtedness to the US in particular. His clothing is the US M1943 battledress, a uniform that worked on a layering system. The outer layers had good properties of wind- and rain-resistance, while inner layers supported warmth. Such a uniform gave fairly substantial winter-weather protection. The US M1 helmet is worn on top of a woolen cap and the weapon is the US 7.62mm M1 Carbine, here fitted with an M4 bayonet. US supplies to the South Korean Army improved as the war went on, tilting the war steadily in South Korea's favor.

SPECIFICATIONS
DATE: 1951
UNIT: Army of the Republic of Korea
RANK: Private
THEATRE: East Asia
LOCATION: South Korea

Guerrilla Fighter, Viet Cong, South Vietnam, 1967

The Soviet AK-47 assault rifle became almost symbolic of the Viet Cong and communist cause during the Vietnam War. Though by no means as sophisticated or accurate as the US 5.56mm M16A1 rifle used by their enemies, it was incredibly dependable, easy to use and could put out ferocious close-quarter firepower. Its reliability was such that many US soldiers used them as an alternative to the M16, which suffered from carbon-fouling and jamming and had to be meticulously cleaned each day. This guerrilla holds an AK-47 and carries ammunition for it in the "ChiCom" chest pouches (for "Chinese Communist" after the nation which pioneered the style) used by many Viet Cong. It was ideal for jungle warfare, as it was comfortable, each pouch holding two AK magazines, plus it was easy to keep clear of foliage when moving through the jungle.

SPECIFICATIONS
DATE: 1967
UNIT: Viet Cong
RANK: Guerrilla Fighter
THEATRE: Southeast Asia
LOCATION: South Vietnam

Lieutenant, 1st Glider Pilot Regiment, Normandy, 1944

This soldier — Lieutenant J.F. Hubble of the 1st Glider Pilot Regiment — is here seen just after the airlanding of British troops, which was undertaken as part of the initial waves of the D-Day invasion force. The treacherous nature of glider landings is suggested by the fiber crash-helmet worn over the Type C flying helmet, while a Type F oxygen mask speaks of the lack of pressurization in the basic Horsa gliders. Though a pilot, Lt. Hubble's uniform shows his allegiance to the airborne forces of the British Army. His camouflage overcoat is the paratrooper's Denison smock, while in his right hand he holds the paras' red beret. To signify that he is a glider pilot, he wears glider wings over his left breast. Glider pilots who weren't members of the army also wore white parachutes or gliders embroidered on the left sleeve in a pale-blue thread.

SPECIFICATIONS
DATE: 6 June 1944
UNIT: 1st Glider Pilot Regiment
RANK: Lieutenant
THEATRE: Northwest Europe
LOCATION: Normandy

Squadron Leader, No. 1 Squadron, RAF, 1982

Harrier GR3 aircraft deployed from Royal Navy aircraft carriers made a seminal contribution to the Falklands War, launching ground-attack missions against Argentine positions and protecting the British Task Force fleet against anti-ship attacks. Here this RAF officer is seen in full flying gear. On the surface he wears an olive, one-piece flying overall, which features clear plastic map pockets on the knees. Beneath is a Mk 10 immersion suit, which would increase survivability should he have to ditch in the freezing South Atlantic, as would the Mk 22 inflatable life-preserver and also a compression suit to help cope with G-forces (the air supply to this is via the hose over the left hip). The blue straps around his legs would pin his legs tight during an ejection and, once landed, the Personal Locator Beacon over his left breast would give rescue forces an exact location that they might be able to work towards.

SPECIFICATIONS
DATE: 1982
UNIT: No.1 Squadron, RAF
RANK: Squadron Leader
THEATRE: South Atlantic
LOCATION: HMS *Invincible*

Lieutenant, US Army, England, 1944

A US Army lieutenant takes a drink just prior to embarking for the D-Day landings on Omaha and Utah beaches. It was common practice in the US Army to paint officer's rank markings on the front of the helmet, despite the threat from snipers. Over his M1941 combat jacket and olive fatigues he wears a mass of equipment for the amphibious landings. The half-inflated pouch centered over his chest is a flotation bag, intended to provide some protection from drowning during the landings. Beneath the bag is an officer's dispatch case containing maps of his objectives. The main priority in equipment apart from these two items is ammunition. He wears a special combat waistcoat with integral ammunition pockets, in addition to his standard belt-hung pouches. His armament is the M1 carbine — here seen slung over the shoulder — and a Colt 11.43mm M1911 pistol in a leather holster on the right hip.

SPECIFICATIONS
DATE: 5 June 1944
UNIT: US Army
RANK: Lieutenant
THEATRE: Northwest Europe
LOCATION: Southern England

Major-General, 82nd Airborne Division, Europe, 1944

The major-general seen here is wearing the M1944 field jacket, popularly known as the "Ike" jacket, after General Eisenhower, the Allied invasion commander. His membership of the 82nd Airborne is denoted by several elements of insignia on this jacket, most distinctly the army paratrooper badge on the left breast, mirrored by a further para badge up on the cap (white set on a navy-blue background). Also featured on the jacket are an infantry combat badge (left breast, beneath the decoration ribbons), a unit citation badge on the right breast — this being made of blue and silver enamel and issued after November 15, 1943 — and the double-A badge of the 82nd on the left sleeve. Rank is indicated by the stripes on the cuff and the stars on the shoulder straps and cap. The cap, a special overseas version, also has gold piping to indicate his general status.

SPECIFICATIONS
DATE: 1944
UNIT: 82nd Airborne Division
RANK: Major-General
THEATRE: Northwest Europe
LOCATION: England

UNITED STATES

Officer, US Women's Army Corps, Pearl Harbor, 1944

This US servicewoman is wearing the cotton summer uniform issued to personnel of the US Women's Army Corps during World War II. It consisted of a dark-olive tunic with open collar, broad lapels and gilt buttons with a matching peaked cap. Underneath the tunic was worn a light khaki blouse and tie. A khaki skirt and a pair of brown leather shoes completed the uniform. The WAC had their own system of insignia. The cap badge was an American eagle, usually less adorned than the standard US Army cap badge, though this officer actually has the regular cap badge with the scroll and motto "E Pluribus Unum". WACs had the letters "US" on the upper collar and the head of the Greek goddess Pallas Athene (goddess of war) beneath. Rank would be shown on the shoulder-straps and, for officers, through the contrasting olive ribbon around the cuff.

SPECIFICATIONS
DATE: December 1944
UNIT: US Women's Army Corps
RANK: Officer
THEATRE: Pacific
LOCATION: Pearl Harbor

Bomber Crewman, 9th Army Air Force, England, 1945

This aviator is a crewman aboard a B-17 Flying Fortress. B-17s were the key US long-range strategic bombers in all theatres except the Pacific, where the B-29 Superfortress was responsible for most of the significant raids against the Japanese mainland. The B-17s bore the brunt of the US policy of daylight bombing against Germany, this policy being altered after hideous losses on the Schweinfurt raid (October 14, 1943) but reinvigorated with the introduction of long-range fighter escorts in 1944. This B-17 crewman is preparing for take-off in early 1945. He is wearing a one-piece flying suit lined with wool and alpaca, over this donning an olive-drab flying jacket with a formation badge on the sleeve. Extra warmth is provided by fleece-lined gloves and zip-on overboots. Headgear consists of an A-11 leather helmet, B-8 flying goggles and an A-10 oxygen mask to cope with altitudes of more than 28,000 feet (8534 m).

SPECIFICATIONS
DATE: February 1945
UNIT: 9th Army Air Force
RANK: Bomber Crewman
THEATRE: Northwest Europe
LOCATION: East Anglia

Marine, US Marine Corps, Inchon, 1950

Deployed to Korea only five years after the end of World War II, this Marine at the Inchon amphibious landings in 1950 has gear worn mainly by US servicemen during the Pacific campaigns. His main uniform items are a set of olive-drab M1944 fatigues in a herringbone-twill material, these being defined by the longitudinal pattern of the cloth, the two large patch pockets on the trousers and the single patch pocket over the left breast with the USMC letters and badge stencilled in black. His helmet is the US M1 with the "beach" camouflage cover, which was worn extensively during the Pacific war. He is carrying ammunition for his M1 7.62mm calibre rifle in his M1923 cartridge belt and also in the cotton bandoliers across his chest, around 200 rounds in total. Visible over his left shoulder is the handle of his bayonet, positioned for easy access to use in hand-to-hand combat situations.

SPECIFICATIONS
DATE: September 1950
UNIT: 1st Marine Division
RANK: Marine
THEATRE: East Asia
LOCATION: Inchon, Korea

Captain, 5th Special Forces Group, Vietnam, 1965

This Special Forces captain — part of the Civilian Irregular Defense Group (CIDG) program training South Vietnamese ethnic groups to fight the Viet Cong — is wearing the standard olive-green fatigues worn by most US soldiers in the early part of the Vietnam War. This initial pattern had slanting patch pockets on the shirt and exposed buttons, as opposed to later patterns, which had horizontal pockets and covered buttons to prevent snagging on undergrowth. However, many SP personnel also wore camouflage outfits, particularly the "Tigerstripe" pattern, which almost became a definer of élite units. His headgear is a green beret with rank bars imposed on the badge (rank bars are also on the right collar). The webbing is the M1956 Load-Carrying Equipment, with an ammunition pack for his 7.62mm M2 Carbine. His boots are canvas-and-leather jungle issue.

SPECIFICATIONS
DATE: 1965
UNIT: CIDG
RANK: Captain
THEATRE: Southeast Asia
LOCATION: South Vietnam

Private, 2nd Marine Division, US Marine Corps, 1991

This US Marine Corps private is seen in the classic six-color "chocolate chip" desert camouflage uniform, made from a 50 percent cotton and 50 percent nylon fabric blend. Designed back in the late 1970s, the uniform was only issued for special desert deployments, hence its use in the 1990–91 Gulf conflict. His backpack is protected by a cover of matching camouflage and he wears a Kevlar anti-fragmentation helmet. A distinctive item of desert wear was the ballistic laser eye protection goggles. These were not only designed to keep out sand and light shell fragments, but also provided ultra-violet protection against the desert sun. He is armed with an M16A2 automatic rifle. His desert boots are a composite leather/canvas design.

SPECIFICATIONS
DATE: February 1991
UNIT: 2nd Marine Division
RANK: Private
THEATRE: Persian Gulf; Operation Desert Storm
LOCATION: Kuwait City

Private, 1st Marine Division (Recon), Iraq, 2003

This private in the 1st Reconnaissance Battalion, 1st US Marine Division, is wearing the Marine Corps Combat Utility Uniform (MCCUU), a standard working/combat uniform that was issued to frontline units since 2002, after field trials the previous year. It now stands as the current battledress uniform of the USMC. The uniform can be rendered in two different computer-generated camouflage patterns known as MARPAT (short for MARine PATtern) — seen here is the Desert pattern, as opposed to the Woodland variant. Ammunition and other items of equipment are held in a tactical vest. The helmet is the new Lightweight Helmet, the lighter and stronger replacement for the previous PASGT helmet system; note the night-vision goggles attachment plate at the front. The firearm is the 5.56mm M4 carbine.

SPECIFICATIONS

DATE: March 2003
UNIT: 1st Recon Battalion, 1st US Marine Division
RANK: Private
THEATRE: Iraq, Operation Iraqi Freedom
LOCATION: Baghdad, Iraq

EOD Operator, 28th Civil Engineer Explosive Ordnance Flight, 2009

Explosive Ordnance Disposal (EOD) personnel require extreme head-to-foot protection to increase their chances of surviving a close-quarters detonation. As seen in this advanced clothing system, ballistic blast plates are concentrated around the chest, abdomen and throat, with a high collar designed to deflect blast away from the head. The blast-resistant helmet features an integral microphone and speakers for ease of communication, while a fan unit helps tackle misting and ventilation. All the materials are made from fire-resistant fabrics. Around the back, an articulated spine protector decreases the chances of spinal injury from blast whiplash. This soldier also wears Kevlar knee pads, so he can kneel in reasonable comfort at the site of the bomb.

SPECIFICATIONS

DATE: September 2009
UNIT: 28th Civil Engineer Explosive Ordnance Flight, USAF
RANK: Airman 1st Class
THEATRE: Iraq, Operation Iraqi Freedom
LOCATION: Baghdad

UNITED STATES

Private, 10th Mountain Division, US Army, Afghanistan, 2010

The Army Combat Uniform (ACU) is the latest adoption by the US Army, replacing the Battle Dress Uniform (BDU) and the Desert Camouflage Uniform (DCU) in 2005. As seen on the soldier here, the most distinctive change was in the camouflage pattern, which is known as Universal Camouflage Pattern (UCP). The UCP mixes slate gray, desert sand and foliage green colors in a pixilated scheme that performs well in a mixture of terrains, from woodland to desert. As well as a change to the camouflage, the uniform introduced 18 distinct structural changes. These include removing the bottom pockets on the jacket and relocating them to the sleeves, so that the soldier could use them while wearing body armor. This soldier is armed with an M4 Carbine, which has replaced the M16 as the battlefield weapon of choice among many branches of the US armed forces.

SPECIFICATIONS
DATE: January 2010
UNIT: 10th Mountain Division
RANK: Private
THEATRE: Afghanistan Operation Enduring Freedom
LOCATION: Kandahar Province

UNIFORMS
1944 TO TODAY

GERMANY
1944 - Private

UNITED STATES
1944 - Major General,
Airborne Division

UNITED KINGDOM
1944 - Lieutenant

UNITED STATES
1944 - Officer,
Women's Army Corps

UNITED STATES
1944 - Army
Air Force Bomber

Major international conflicts involving the United States

WORLD WAR II 1939 -1945

IRAQ
1991 - Private,
Iraqi Army

UNITED STATES
1991 - Private,
Marine Corps

PERSIAN GULF WAR 1990 -1991

COLD WAR 1945 -1991

WEAPONS OF WAR

FEATURED UNIFORMS TIMELINE

This timeline features notable advancements in
military technologies by influential nations worldwide.

UNITED STATES
1951 - Private,
US Airborne Forces

SOUTH KOREA
1951 - Private

UNITED STATES
1965 - Captain,
Special Forces

SOUTH VIETNAM
1967 - Guerrilla Fighter,
Viet Cong

KOREAN WAR 1950 -1953

VIETNAM WAR 1954 - 1975

COLD WAR 1945 -1991

AFGHANISTAN
2001 - Guerrilla Fighter,
Taliban Militia

UNITED STATES
2003 - Private,
Marine Corps

IRAQ
2003 - Fighter,
Fedayeen Saddam Militia

UNITED STATES
2010 - Private,
Army

AFGHANISTAN WAR 2001 - PRESENT

IRAQ WAR 2003 - 2011

Glossary

breech loading
loading ammunition in a chamber that is in the rear portion of the barrel instead of the muzzle

camouflage
an inconsistent pattern of colors and shapes that blends in the with the surroundings

casualties
any person in a military unit who has been injured or died of wounds or disease in a hostile (battle) or non-hostile (disease)setting

Cold War
political tension and military rival between two nations or factions that has not become a full-scale war

disparate
widely different or unalike

ergonomic
designed to be easily and efficiently

forage cap
a military cap worn with fatigues

guerilla
a person or small, independent unit that participates in irregular warfare in territory controlled by a hostile force

ideological
goals and ideals that characterizes the thinking of a group, culture, or nation

Janissaries
neither freemen nor ordinary slaves, the Janissaries were the first Ottoman army to wear a uniform

Kit
clothes and equipment used by a soldier

logistics
the planning and organizing an event that involves many people

proxy war
a conflict instigated or supported by countries that aren't directly involved in the fighting

regimental
military unit that is usually made of several groups of soldiers called battalions

Further Information

Websites

http://science.howstuffworks.com/military-camouflage.htm
Find out more about military camouflage and the science behind it.

http://www.surplusandadventure.com/shop/home/product-information/camouflage/military-camouflage.html
View the different camouflage designs used on uniforms, ships, and vehicles.

http://camopedia.org/index.php?title=USA
The Camouflage Encyclopedia shows historical camouflage patterns.

http://www.theatlantic.com/technology/archive/2011/06/a-brief-history-of-military-camouflage/240291
See how military camouflage has changed throughout history.

Books

Brayley, Martin J. *Camouflage Uniforms.* Crowood Press, 2009.
Color images of worldwide armed forces uniforms that were designed to conceal troops in various environments.

Newark, Tim. *The Book of Camouflage: The Art of Disappearing.* Osprey Publishing, 2013.
View images of military personnel in camouflaged uniforms from around the world.

Rottman, Gordon and Peter Dennis. *World War II Tactical Camouflage Techniques* (Elite), 2013.
Learn about the use of camouflage for the person, equipment, and weapons.

Borsarello, J.F. *Camouflage Uniforms of Eurpean and NATO Armies: 1945 to the Present*, Schiffer Publishing, 2007.
A comprehensive reference illustrating camouflage uniforms of more than forty armies.

Index of Uniform Profile Pages